Two Places At A Time

by Doris Diana Marin

Illustrated by Kendall Marie Jackson

Two Places At A Time
is dedicated to
Noah, Genevieve, Maya, Mason and Jonah,
who fill my life with joy.
With greatest love, Nana Doris.

Author: Doris Diana Marin
Illustrated by: Kendall Marie Jackson

ISBN: Softcover 978-1-4535-8743-0
Hardcover 978-1-4535-8744-7

This book was printed in the United States of America.

To order additional copies of this book, contact:
Xlibris Corporation
1-888-795-4274
www.Xlibris.com
Orders@Xlibris.com

If I could be two places at a time,

I'd spend my time with you.

I'd be with you
all day

and night,

And teach you

all that's right.

If I could travel here

and there

We'd be together everywhere.

I have a playground there

and here,

My time with you

I hold most dear.

Time with you
would just stand still,

With happiness,

my day would fill.

If I could be
two places at a time,

I'd be right here with you.

About the Illustrator: Kendall Marie Jackson, designer and illustrator, is known for her whimsical, lovable drawings that captivate adults and children alike. Kendall has a background in Apparel Design and Marketing and has always had a passion for creating imaginative illustration as well as cheerful home goods and personal accessories. Many of her designs are available under the TootieEstelle Designs label at TOOTIEESTELLE.com

www.ingramcontent.com/pod-product-compliance
Ingram Content Group UK Ltd.
Pitfield, Milton Keynes, MK11 3LW, UK
UKHW060115300726
14090UKWH00002B/205
9781453587430